THE MEDIA

ADVERTISING

David Lusted

The Media

Advertising
Book Publishing
Cinema
Magazines
The Pop Music Business
Newspapers
Radio
Television and Video

This book is dedicated to Cath and Jim

Series designer: David Armitage
Series editor: Susannah Foreman
Cover: *Neon signs at Piccadilly Circus, London*

First published in 1988 by
Wayland (Publishers) Ltd
61 Western Road, Hove
East Sussex BN3 1JD, England

Phototypeset by Direct Image Photosetting, Hove
Printed in Italy by G. Canale & C.S.p.A., Turin
Bound in France by AGM

British Library Cataloguing in Publication Data

Lusted, David
  Advertising — (The media)
  1. Advertising
  I. Title   II. Series
  659.1   HF5821

ISBN 1-85210-237-3

Contents

Advertising surrounds us. Giant posters and neon-lit slogans look down upon us from prime sites on busy streets of every city in the world. Advertisements — ads, for short — interrupt television programmes and are often made at a cost greater than the programmes they disturb. No newspaper or magazine can be read without coming across ads, which often take up whole pages. Many newspapers and magazines cannot exist without the revenue they receive from selling space to advertisers.

Advertising is big business — very big business. In 1983, more than twenty companies spent over £13,000,000 each on advertising their products in Britain alone. In the same year, advertising agencies — companies who make money by selling other companies and their products — earned over £54,000,000 each. One

Right *Advertising fills every available space in New York's Times Square, just as it does in the big tourist spots of every major city in the world.*

British agency, Saatchi and Saatchi, topped the list with an income of £114,000,000. Because so much money is involved in advertising, it is not surprising that it is a subject that arouses a great many differences of opinion.

Most people involved in advertising think of it both as a service to advertisers, those who have goods to sell, and to consumers, those who buy the products advertised. You can be critical of that simple idea, however, without necessarily being opposed to the concept of advertising.

Many people disagree with advertising. They say it is unnecessary since any product, especially if it is useful and of good quality, will sell itself. Advertisers would probably say this is nonsense; that products will not sell at all unless people are made aware of their existence. This is what advertising means; to draw attention to something you have to sell.

In this sense, advertising is inevitable. Everybody advertises. Each time we open our mouths to speak, or dress to leave our homes

Below *The table shows how much money is spent on advertising and where it is spent in the press and in other media in Britain.*

Total advertising expenditure by media

	1960		1975		1980		1986	
	£m	%	£m	%	£m	%	£m	%
National newspapers	64	19.0	162	16.8	426	16.7	844	16.5
Regional newspapers	77	23.8	283	29.3	640	25.7	1101	21.5
Magazines and periodicals	40	12.4	79	8.2	192	7.5	274	5.4
Trade and technical	31	9.6	86	8.9	214	8.4	373	7.3
Other	17	5.2	69	7.2	212	8.3	544	10.6
TOTAL PRESS	229	70.9	679	70.2	1684	65.9	3136	61.3
TV	72	22.3	236	24.4	692	27.1	1675	32.7
Poster and transport	16	5.0	35	3.6	107	4.2	196	3.8
Cinema	5	1.5	7	0.7	18	0.7	19	0.4
Radio	1	0.3	10	1.0	54	2.1	91	1.8
TOTAL	323	100.0	967	100.0	2555	100.0	5117	100.0

Everyone 'advertises' through the image they project of themselves by their appearance. Youth sub-cultures in particular draw attention with their spectacular and surprising look.

we are drawing attention to the ways we would like others to think of us. We are promoting a product, just like an ad does, but in this case the product we are promoting is ourselves.
Many critics of advertising disagree with the way ads use language emotionally to persuade people to buy things they often may not need or cannot really afford. Others object to the false promises of the comfortable ways of living or ideal relationships offered by the ads. It is certainly true that ads deal with dreams and fantasies, but less certain that we associate the products advertised with these dreams and

fantasies in the ways the advertiers may intend. The same argument goes for the language of ads. If we all know that ads are seeking to sell us something, are we also not aware that their language seeks to manipulate us? And if we know we are being manipulated, how successful can they be?

These arguments about the underhand and dishonest work of advertising may be correct, to a greater or lesser extent. But they are less persuasive when we remember that we *know* what the purpose of advertising is. Most of us do not rush off to buy a product when we see an ad for it, although, of course, we may be reminded of it when we see it or wish to buy something like it. And here the argument becomes different. Does advertising work at the point where it matters most — when we are consumers, out shopping or leafing through mail order catalogues? If so, *how* does it work? At such times, does advertising work in ways we cannot be conscious of? (Since we are unconscious of it, how could we ever know?)

There are no clear answers to such questions. What is clear, though, is that you do not have to be an advertiser to accept that advertising is inevitable. Most people know very well what the intentions of ads are and how they are intended to work.

Still, it is possible to be concerned, not about advertising itself, but about the way some groups have more money and power to advertise than others. Because most of us are in this unequal relationship with the advertising industry, we can be its victims at least as much as its beneficiaries.

At some time in our lives, for instance, most of us will want to sell something, like a bicycle we no longer need or an unwanted gift. We can advertise by putting a card in a newsagents' shop window or by paying for space in the classified section of a local newspaper. We are unlikely to pay an advertising agency to make an ad to go on television or on the front page of a newspaper. It would cost us more than the value of the item we have to sell.

Big companies with the means to pay for expensive forms of advertising are able to draw attention to their goods much more successfully than we can. We are selling just one item whereas companies are selling their product all the time; they need to advertise continuously whereas we will probably advertise just once or twice.

Once a company begins to use advertising, it cannot *afford* to stop or else its competitors might have the advantage. The pressure is on to advertise more products than one's competitors. That is why successful companies grow ever bigger, diversifying into new and different ranges of products and even advertising themselves.

Advertising has now become very important. The advertising industry penetrates all

Large sums of money are required to pay for the media, ideas and design skills that companies like Araldite can command to advertise their products.

Companies such as the Coca Cola company spend large amounts of money to keep their product in the public eye.

aspects of our lives. It affects how we think of ourselves, what we do with our time, how decisions are made and how we use our money.

Some groups of people try to change aspects of the advertising system. These people are outraged by ads that use images of themselves in ways they find offensive. In addition to voicing complaints to the appropriate authorities, some people take matters into their own hands by adding witty lines of graffiti to posters in the streets. In Australia, a militant anti-smoking lobby has been defacing posters on a spectacular scale for many years.

There are many ways of thinking about advertising — as a concept, as an industry, as a way of life — and many more competing views and ways of responding to it. The best views and responses are informed by some sense of the history of advertising and how it is organized today.

Graffiti on hoardings: mindless vandalism or one way to overcome the lack of money or power to answer advertising back?

2 The history of advertising

The roots of advertising lie in public announcements such as the contests between gladiators in the arenas of Ancient Rome, public executions in medieval Europe and 'Wanted' criminals on the American frontier. 'Posting' — literally, hanging notices from trees or posts — was an early form of the advertising posters we now see on street hoardings and billboards.

Advertisements first appeared in early English news sheets, in the middle of the seventeenth century. These primitive newspapers or mercuries (named after the first of them, *Mercurius Britannicus*) carried ads for books, lost horses or patent medicines. The ads remind us of modern advertising not only in their selling intentions but also in their distinctive use of language. Information is

The earliest advertisements were public announcements like this reward poster for the outlaw Frank James of the Jesse James Gang on the American frontier of the 1860s.

REWARD

**$15,000 REWARD
FRANK JAMES**

DEAD or ALIVE

$25,000 REWARD FOR JESSE JAMES
$5000 Reward for any Known Member of the James Band

SIGNED

ST. LOUIS MIDLAND RAILROAD

The Last Week

THE MOST WONDERFUL PERFORMANCE
EVER EXHIBITED IN EUROPE, AT
89, STRAND.

THE YOUNG NATIVE OF LYONS,

Jeane Rosalie Raymon,

AGED 17 YEARS,

BORN WITHOUT ARMS,

Of whom already many Editors in Paris, St. Petersburg, Dresden, Vienna, Berlin, Hamburgh, Dantzic, Prague, and other Newspapers, has been mentioned, and has had the honour to exhibit her wonderful performances before all the chief Nobility and Gentry on the Continent, has just arrived in London, and solicits the patronage of the Nobility and the Public in general. She is of a lively disposition, conversant, and intelligent, having the art to use her feet for the want of her arms. Further particulars we leave to the learned and generous public.

JEANE ROSALIE RAYMON,

From Lyons, in France, has, besides her Fine Form, a great number of Talents worth seeing: she does with her feet, with the greatest cleverness, several kinds of work, such as Writing, Cutting, Drawing, Knitting, Embroidering, Threads a Needle, and Sews, Nets Purses with Pears, Neck Chains, Watch Ribbons, &c. She eats and drinks, and plays Cards and Dominos, Loads and Fires a Pistol, &c. &c. This young Woman is very interesting, and well worthy to be seen, and executes all her accomplishments with such delicacy, that the most scrupulous eye cannot be offended by her exhibition.

~~Front Seats 2s. Back Seats 1s. Children Half-price.~~

Front Seats 1 Shilling Back Sixpence

delivered in a way that arouses our attention and not merely alerts us.

In the case of some early products, a sensational language hardly seemed necessary to sell them. Freak shows in travelling fairs were common, for instance. They featured such sights as 'a man half human, half bear, with a dog growing from its back'. With so incredible an attraction, why was it thought important to add that it had 'to be seen without a moment's delay!'

These first printed advertisements were often hard to distinguish from the body of the newspaper. The typeface was the same, and the advertisements were not boxed off but merged into news stories. This lack of distinction between news and ads, whether innocent or intended, was found to cause problems, but certainly seemed to work in the advertisers' favour. So the need for regulation of the advertisers' arts was recognized from early times.

By the end of the seventeenth century advertising had become an important part of the wealth of European nations. Merchants returning from travels to African and Asian countries brought back new foods and other goods. Tea and coffee arrived, exotic fruit and spices, new cloth such as lace and calico. Humans were part of this trade, too; the slave trade from Africa began at this time.

During this period advertising developed and many of the central features of the industry were established. With completely unfamiliar products, advertising was crucial to *create* a demand for them, rather than to satisfy a demand that already existed. Traders had to advertise to convince their consumers to buy coffee beans in order to make a delicious new drink. In the same way now, companies — the traders of today — advertise to convince us that, for example, instant coffee is a more convenient preparation for drinking. Demand is created today not just for new products but for different forms of old products.

Left *A handbill advertising one of the popular 'freak' shows of Victorian England, ghoulish for its exploitation of handicapped people, and fascinating for its handwritten amendment reducing the admission price — to compensate perhaps for lack of public interest?*

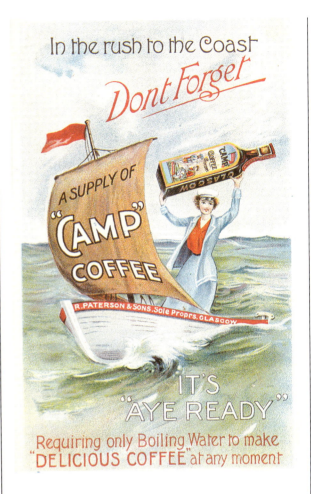

An early twentieth century ad for Camp coffee essence offers an early example of the modern advertiser's skills: a catchy slogan and eye-catching graphic design.

By the beginning of the nineteenth century the number and range of goods for sale was rising rapidly, because of increased production as a result of the industrial revolution. Advertising increased at the same time, and even more when a government tax on advertising was abolished in 1853. By the end of the century, much of the modern advertiser's craft had been established. Early versions of slogans such as 'Butt's Beer is Best', appeared and more eye-catching typefaces, illustrations and designs developed.

By the turn of the century, two things combined to establish a pattern for advertising as we recognize it today. First, the advertising agency was formed; a company who made their money by producing ads for other companies.

VOLUNTEERS WANTED!

1776! **1861!**

AN ATTACK UPON WASHINGTON ANTICIPATED ! !

THE COUNTRY TO THE RESCUE !

A REGIMENT FOR SERVICE

UNDER THE FLAG  OF THE UNITED STATES

IS BEING FORMED IN JEFFERSON COUNTY.

 NOW IS THE TIME TO BE ENROLLED !

Left *The Pears soap campaign began in 1886. It was the first to use a famous painting and high quality colour reproduction to advertise an everyday product by associating it with wealth and luxury.*

Above *The woodcut illustration, bold headline and sentimental copy of this 1861 recruitment poster demonstrates the last period of information-led advertising techniques.*

Second, newspapers began to give separate space for display ads, which are boxed-in combinations of artwork (picture) and copy (text or words), like the famous Pears Soap advertisement.

By the start of the First World War in Europe

in 1914, advertising had become a profession, employing thousands of people in jobs across the nations of the industrialized world. It had also become an industry, with its own methods of producing, circulating and displaying ads by an increasing variety of methods.

14

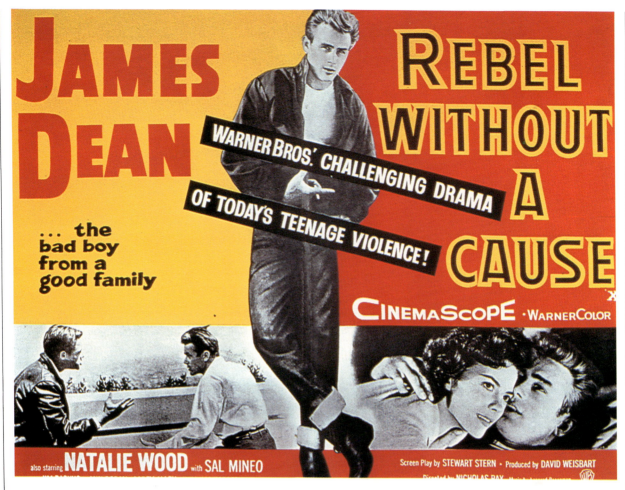

Above *In response to the 1950s' consumer boom advertisers developed direct, sensational styles of communication, as in this film poster for teenage cinema-goers.*

Principles of the relatively new science of psychology were also adapted to sell products more effectively. Emotional appeals, scare tactics and implausible promises became part of the advertiser's armoury.

Advertising expanded greatly after the Second World War ended in 1945. The post-war consumer boom of the 1950s saw many more products and many more outlets for advertising. Women's magazines mushroomed along with the demand for domestic goods such as washing machines and personal items like cosmetics and jewellery. For the first time, young people had money to spend on leisure

Left *The bold, immediate impact of the message in this Second World War Canadian recruitment poster contrasts strongly with the poster on page 13.*

activities and clothing. Magazines and films for the new 'teenage' market became major vehicles for advertising by the early 1960s.

The biggest boost to advertising expenditure came from the new medium of television. American television has always been financed by sponsorship — companies paying for programmes to be produced and the right for their 'messages' to be featured during them. In Britain, advertising did not come to television until 1955 when a commercial channel was established. Unlike the American model, commercial television in Britain is financed through advertisers buying time, rather than programmes, through which to advertise their wares. Advertisers in Britain, therefore, are not associated with particular programmes. This is one of the reasons why ads on British television are considered more attractive and cost much more to make than their American counterparts.

Advertising by sponsorship is an increasing

The London marathon has been sponsored by many of the biggest companies. Runners carry their individual sponsor's name on their vests.

practice. Events may be specially staged to attract the attention of journalists and broadcasters. Tobacco firms sponsor sporting events so that the names of their products will be displayed on football jerseys or racing cars; chocolate bar companies give grants to touring arts groups and exhibitions so that their names will be mentioned and caught by the cameras.

Sponsorship costs are no more than advertising costs. The main advantage is that this form of indirect advertising may not appear to the public to be advertising at all. Moreover, sponsors may benefit from appearing to be doing generous and charitable work. Most companies now sponsor on some scale, realizing the advantages of keeping their names as well as the names of their products in the public eye. Some companies may even be prepared to sponsor minority-interest activities if it associates their names with high-minded

causes. Mobil Oil, for instance, sponsored a series of television programmes called PBS Masterpiece Theatre in the USA, and a programme of film restoration for the National Film Archive in Britain.

Sponsorship is a form of indirect advertising, a popular new practice that is likely to increase even more. Another technique uses advertorials, news 'stories' in the form of press releases or special supplements paid for in newspapers. What appears as a series of articles about computers or Japan turns out, on closer inspection, to be part of an extensive advertising supplement for a particular company's computers or Japan's tourist attractions.

As the variety of forms of advertising increases, so every agency in a society feels it necessary to advertise. Political parties, charities, religious groups and trade unions once neglected advertising but now find it essential. (Television in Britain, however, has not caught up with the USA — 'political' advertising is banned, so trade unions and groups such as the Campaign for Nuclear Disarmament and Greenpeace cannot advertise on television.)

As the number of new media outlets develop in the late twentieth century, there is no doubt that advertising will increase and change. Outlets such as cable and satellite television may not see many changes in the forms of advertising, but new developments such as teletext and home computers will most certainly demand changes in the ways advertisers seek to command our attention. Whatever happens in the future, the power of the video screen in our homes is assured for some time.

Advertising has developed to keep pace with the greater number and diversity of media outlets over the centuries. What started in small and primitive ways has been transformed into a complex and wealthy industry with the power to maintain its prominence into the foreseeable future.

Like many non-commercial organizations, the ecology- and environment-minded Greenpeace has learned the value of advertising techniques, even if it sometimes falls foul of bans on 'political' advertising.

3 How advertising is organized

You may remember the case of advertising your bicycle in the first chapter. Three people would be involved in this. There would be you, the newsagent in whose window you displayed your card and the person who bought your bike. These three roles and the relationship between them are reproduced in the advertising industry, too. They are: the advertiser — the producers of goods who spend money to have them advertised (like you, paying the newsagent for the hire of part of their window); the media — who own and control the publications, poster sites and broadcasting channels that carry ads (like your newsagent), and the consumer who buys the goods advertised (like the person who buys your bargain bike). But in the industry there is a fourth role too — the advertising agency, which produces advertising for other companies.

When you wrote your advertisement, you probably designed the card yourself, with the aid of perhaps a few coloured pens and maybe even a photograph of your bike. Advertising agencies employ professional staff who take over this role. They would offer more than a designer, however, for their work is not just to produce a single ad like yours, but to plan a whole advertising campaign.

The process of advertising begins with the advertiser, who employs the agency to design a campaign. The agency employs the media that exposes it, and finally the consumer receives it.

Companies who produce goods constantly search for new ways of selling them. They need to keep making money to pay their employees, their shareholders and their management. If a company were a monopoly (that is, if it had the exclusive control of a product) it would need do no more than draw attention to the product it

The advertising agency decides whether to place advertisements in the press, on television or on hoardings in prominent positions.

GET
GET
THE
THE
MAX
TASTE

Brands like Maxwell House become household names through constant advertising. Campaigns come and go, subtly changing the brand image to keep a place in the coffee-buying markets.

alone provided. But most companies compete with others that are producing the same or a similar product. They advertise their brand of product in an effort to sell more than their competitors. This is why leading companies constantly advertise to maintain or even increase their share of sales of a like product —

why Coca-Cola and Pepsi advertise a comparable fizzy drink formula, and why Nescafé, Birds and Maxwell House advertise similar instant coffee.

When a company wants to launch a new brand name or to boost sales of an existing brand, it needs to find the best ways of reaching those groups of people most likely to buy it. This is not as simple as it may sound. Obviously, advertising, say, a new brand of chocolate bar has to appeal to people who enjoy eating chocolate. But many people only buy one or a limited range of bars and others have no preference. And why should any of these people give up the bars they already buy?

This is where the advertising agency comes in. The agency will find out which group of people will want to buy a particular brand of product. This is called meeting demand. Some agencies will even be employed to seek out groups who could be persuaded to buy a product they are unaware of. This is called creating demand. Groups may be distinguished by any number of combinations of disposable income and lifestyle, class, sex, race or age. The permutations are considerable. Any combination for a particular brand is called a market. Seeking information about them is therefore termed market research.

Once the agency discovers which market(s) they want to reach, they have to decide on the most appropriate media to reach it. There would be no point in advertising your bike in the window of a shop far away from your home. Likewise, no local business, such as a garage or a plumber, will advertise beyond the area where their customers live. They will advertise in a local newspaper or on regional television. On a larger scale, an oil company will advertise in the national press and on television since everyone can buy their brand of petrol from a local garage. Availability of a brand, then, determines where and on what media it is advertised.

The nature of the market for the brand is another important criterion. Advertising a labourer's job in a business magazine, or women's underwear during children's television would not make much sense. There are more appropriate media with which to reach the people you want, to target your market.

Advertisers do not necesssarily seek the largest market. Small but wealthy markets can be even more lucrative. Advertisers may sell fewer numbers of high quality, expensive

Below *Competing brands of coffee campaign in similar ways. This Nescafé ad breaks new ground by offering the idea of coffee as an iced drink in its aim to attract a younger market.*

Right *Benetton broke into the upper end of the children's clothes market by targeting its campaign for expensive, fashionable styles at selected children's and women's magazines.*

UNITED FASHIONS OF BENETTON

PURE NEW WOOL

LEAPS AHEAD!

ESSO EXTRA

THE GREAT PETROL WITH 6 EXTRAS

products but their profit on each sale may be higher than on cheaper ones. Using the media of 'serious' newspapers or minority-interest television programmes will target these markets precisely.

A considerable number of advertising agencies are owned by American companies. There are 700 agencies in Britain, most of them specializing in television advertising, since the largest profits are to be made there. In Britain it costs nearly £40,000 for a 60-second spot during peak-time viewing (6 pm to 10.35 pm) but the world record goes to the American NBC

*Over several generations, Esso has stayed true to its tiger character. Nonetheless, the tiger has changed its appearance over different campaigns — the powerful creature in the colour painting (**above**) becomes a fun-loving cartoon 'tiger in your tank' (**opposite, top**) and, most recently, we have the regal figure pounding through the surf.*

Cost of Advertising in British Press

Newspaper	Price	Circulation	Cost of Full Page Advertisement
Daily Express	22p	1,713,284	£18,865.00
Daily Telegraph	25p	1,132,121	£24,640.00
The Independent	25p	288,660	£7,500.00
The Scotsman	25p	95,337	£5,500.00
The Sun	18p	4,012,388	£23,562.00
The Times	25p	450,385	£11,500.00

The table indicates how much more must be paid for advertising in newspapers not only with the most readers but also with the wealthiest readers.

during peak-time viewing (6 pm to 10.35 pm) but the world record goes to the American NBC network for receiving nearly $600,000 per minute for advertising during the transmission of the Super Bowl. Although costs are far less during off-peak times, television advertising is still much more expensive than newspaper advertising.

An agency is contracted by an advertiser who is thereafter termed a client or an account. Once an agency has decided on the best media for its chosen market, it turns its attention to the brand image. A creative director is employed to decide on the image she or he wants to create for the product. This may include the design of the packet for the breakfast cereal or the colour of the car to be used in the ad. Copywriters produce copy — the text — and art directors commission photographs or film for the advertisement.

The agency then presents a variety of ideas for the campaign to the client. Negotiating this can take a long time but, once agreed, ads are made and space is bought on whatever media the agency has decided on: television, radio and billboards, or newspapers, magazines and cinemas.

The life of a campaign can vary. Political parties may be interested in a campaign lasting only a few weeks — the life of an election campaign. Some companies use the basic idea of a campaign for many years and even take it

with them when they change agency. The Esso Oil Company tiger has been around in different forms for over twenty years. In the USA Aunt Jemimah has been selling pancakes for nearly sixty years.

Advertising is as competitive a business as any other industry and agencies fight hard to gain and keep profitable accounts. In Britain, one of the top agencies, Saatchi and Saatchi, fought off an American competitor to keep the Conservative Party account through three general elections from 1979-87. Another agency, J. Walter Thompson, were shocked to lose a £6,000,000 account with Guinness, but quickly won back their position close to the top ten of advertising agents with a new client, ICL.

When a campaign is over, an agency's account executive can claim as much as 15 per cent of the total cost of the campaign as agency profit.

Obviously, it must benefit advertisers to advertise and to employ agencies to plan campaigns. In the end, though, it is the consumer who pays, since the cost of the campaign has to be passed on through the purchase price of the goods we buy. About 15 per cent of a purchase price is attributed directly to advertising costs, so there is an obvious equation between the amount of profit agencies make and the prices consumers pay. As consumers, do you and I pay unwillingly for an unnecessary and wasteful service? Or do we pay willingly for the information, excitement and laughter produced by the ads of the agencies' creative staff?

4 Advertising, consumers and audiences

We all know that the purpose of advertising is to sell brands of products. We also know that if it did not succeed in this purpose, it would not exist. Yet not all advertising succeeds, nor is it necessarily the case that we, as people who look at and listen to advertising, use it for the purpose intended by the advertiser.

To the advertising industry, we are consumers: potential buyers who have to be made into actual buyers. Many advertising campaigns fail to increase the sales of their products, and many campaigns to launch new products have been withdrawn and re-devised several times before meeting success. Sometimes, new products are abandoned after several different campaigns have failed in their objective. There can be many reasons for failure. The campaign can be poor, the market poorly researched, the wrong media chosen or the relation between any of these can meet unexpected problems. More often than not, however, everything can be right and still not stimulate consumers to buy.

Advertisers know that advertising is no science; apparently good products, which have been well advertised, may fail to meet with a response. As consumers, we are not as predictable as advertisers may claim. Indeed, some critics argue that not only is chance the most important factor in the success of a campaign, but some products are successful despite their campaigns.

This ad from the campaign for TU cosmetics was thought to be unsuccessful. One reason for this was that what was being sold, what TU might do for you, was too vague.

This is from the replacement TU campaign which was more successful. Targeted at 'ordinary girls' aged 19-30, it set out more clearly what TU could do for them.

Tu. How to hold a conversation without saying a word.

All you need is Tu. On your lips. On your nails.

The shades are honest. Extrovert. Never shy. 55p for a lipstick. 55p for a nail colour.

Just stroke on an exciting Tu lip colour.

Then match it with a glossy Tu nail colour.

The rest is up to you. Others will get the message and you needn't say a word.

Tu. The intimate you. The seductive you.

It's a complete range of highly coloured expression.

Fifteen matching lip and nail colours in plain and pearl that say exactly what is on your mind.

Even if you are too shy to say it out loud.

Those eyes so helpless and appealing.

Your eyes are the eyes of a little girl lost. Sort of helpless and don't know what to do.

All you need is Tu. The range that puts a flashbang look in your eyes.

A glance will pin him to the wall. Make him crawl.

Whispering shadows mix with wild colours in a frenzy of emotional hues.

Eight Tu product ranges that let your eyes say what your lips would never dare. Fourteen plain and pearl Shades in single powder shadow packs and One Plain/One Pearl duo packs.

Super soft Stickers. Swivel eye shadow sticks for a subtle suggestion of colour.

And Kohl pencils to outline your intentions.

He'll get the message. And a page in your little black book.

One day will flash and send him crashing through the ceiling.

One way of understanding the chance factor lies in the power we, as consumers, have to make or break an advertising campaign. Unlike advertisers, we think of ourselves as consumers for only part of the time. Our views of advertising may be very different to those of the advertising industry. We are not so much consumers as 'audiences' for advertising.

When we go out into the streets, we may hardly be aware of the advertising around us. Billboards, posters, shop windows, carrier bags displaying shop names — any number of places and spaces can carry ads. They fill our environment in a way that makes us think of advertising much as we think about breathing — as a quite natural event. Similarly, we rarely read ads in newspapers or magazines with the kind of attention we give to the newspaper articles around them. On television, too, the advertising break during programmes is the time in which we stretch out, talk more attentively to friends or family, or leave the room briefly before returning to pick up the threads of the programme where it left off. We probably have very general impressions of the advertising with which we are confronted.

This may explain one of the puzzles that seems regularly to confront advertisers — how do people miss the point or meaning of a particular campaign? Often, advertisers find that people tested after watching or reading a campaign have failed to understand what the ad was for or what it was saying about a product. Responses like this can mystify advertisers or, worse, make them think that consumers are stupid.

It may be, however, that consumers wish to know only so much as they choose to, and that they pick up only fleeting impressions about ads. It is the quality of their attention that determines how much of an ad they need to understand. Rather than being stupid we are being selective, and actively attending only to those ads that arouse us.

Advertising can bring bold colours, bright designs, witty phrases and exciting images into our daily lives. And we can use advertising if we think of it like this in ways not directly important to advertisers. Standing in London's Piccadilly Circus or New York's Times Square late at night, the changing neon light advertising

At night time in the major cities of the world, as here in Kowloon, the visual spectacle of light and colour can be overwhelming.

displays can be spectacular. Some American and Australian billboards are on a scale so large and of a visual quality so stunning that they can be breath-taking. Particular campaigns can also give pleasure in this way. In Britain in 1986, a match company called Bryant and May rekindled interest in black and white .

The Swan Vesta matches campaign displayed beautiful black and white photographs of early Hollywood stars, such as Veronica Lake, in many British towns.

photography by displaying large portraits of early Hollywood stars in many towns.

Indeed, some billboards in the USA became so celebrated that groups of fans fought to have them protected long after their advertising function had disappeared. On such occasions, the interests of commerce overcame objections and the billboards concerned were always replaced.

Certain campaigns have also remained in many people's memories long after they were dropped, like Burmah Shave in the USA and the Guinness toucan in Britain. The war enlistment posters of Lord Kitchener and, later, Uncle Sam pointing a finger to implore 'Your Country Needs You' remain familiar images even to people who never saw the originals. People enjoy some of the witty and puzzling ads in the Benson and Hedges cigarettes campaign, even those who dislike smoking. People who never drink beer can enjoy the television ads for Carling Black Label lager. People who would never wear jeans nonetheless talk nostalgically about the ads for Levi 501s because of their use of early rock music and subtly romantic images.

Some of the most memorable campaigns have borrowed freely from films and television programmes, variety shows and comics to tell short stories, make jokes or in other ways make us sad, smile or simply interested. The Oxo family is reminiscent of soap opera, the Peugeot campaign uses suspense and shock devices like film thrillers, and the Skol lager ads are a series of jokes with punch lines. Ads vie with other forms of fiction and popular entertainment to gain our attention. Television ads are short, and posters may be seen only for fleeting moments as we drive past them. They have to attract our interest and make their point fast, and advertisers have developed design skills to do just that. Ads tell stories we are interested in, in ways that attract our immediate attention.

A final way in which we might use ads is, simply, for ourselves. We might see something

Below *Consumers have been told they can 'be sure of Shell' long enough for many people to be able to hum the tune that accompanied the slogan in the 1950s campaign.*

Right *Everyone knows what happened to the* Titanic *when it met an iceberg on its maiden voyage. An Australian newspaper wittily uses that knowledge some 75 years later in this ad.*

EVERYWHERE YOU GO

THE QUAY - APPLEDORE

BRYNHILD PARKER.

YOU CAN BE SURE OF SHELL

IT'S SAFER THAN GOING TO THE AUSTRALIAN STOCK MARKET.

'Dancing on the Titanic'. A report in tomorrow's Times on Sunday that every Australian shareholder or potential shareholder must read. So make sure you keep up with the Times... on Sunday.

29

of ourselves in an ad, how we live now or as we would like to think of ourselves. We can identify with many of the characters or find models of how others might think of themselves. Through such forms of recognition we can indirectly learn from ads.

All of this can be taking place regardless of the messages intended by advertisers. Asking what we use ads for gives many different

The Andrex campaign wrapped puppies in toilet rolls and us in romantic fantasies of childhood memories, as in this soft-focus echo of Alice in Wonderland, doll's houses and nursery rhymes.

answers to asking what advertising is for. But what about the messages? Clearly some ads, at least, must have the desired effect of encouraging us to buy. Do they? If so, how?

5 Looking closely at advertisements

All advertisements, in whatever medium, share certain characteristics. They all feature the brand name, usually as part of the eye-catching slogan like 'Drinka Pinta Milka Day' or 'Electricity — Clean Simplicity'. The slogans, in large and bold typography, are usually the first thing our eyes are drawn to in an ad. A second characteristic is the body of the ad, the factual copy, telling more about the product in smaller type than the slogan. In a television or cinema ad, the slogan may be spoken and written on the screen, while the copy is usually spoken or sung. Third, most ads have some form of illustration, usually a photograph or piece of artwork, or sometimes in the form of a graph or table of figures.

These basic characteristics combine to produce a brand image or product identification, an idea that projects an image of the product the advertisers want us to keep in mind. The Marlboro cigarette cowboy is a good example.

He has been associating the brand with rugged, male outdoor activity, as well as more abstract ideas such as freedom, nature and the individual, for many years. The Marlboro cowboy has been a successful brand image for such a long time not least because it precisely describes not one but many intended markets. The markets are male, but men of many different ages and social positions, each see something of themselves in the product. Sure enough, the Marlboro packet is bought overwhelmingly by men. Compare this brand image with Virginia Slims cigarettes, with their pastel shades, thin wisps of smoke and hints of special occasions and romantic meetings. Does it come as a surprise to learn that this brand is bought overwhelmingly by women?

The brand image will contain clues to the market the product is intended for. No bar of soap will be advertised for its cleaning properties alone. An ad will tell us immediately if it is soap for men with dirty hands, women with dry skin, the cheapest way to keep the family clean or an exclusive way to make the bathroom smell good. The copy, design and brand image of every ad combine to tell us who the product is aimed at.

Every ad tells a story, even if it is a very

There is no need to spell out the brand name of this fast food when its image of wholesome fare for active kids and their busy mums is so very familiar.

minimal story. The ads for Charles Atlas body-building equipment, especially familiar in the 1950s, are strip cartoons in the form of a typical 'before and after' story; the skinny weakling becoming the strong man attractive to women. The 'before and after' story has now become so familiar that jokes are made about it, as in the Heineken beer campaign which 'refreshes the parts other beers cannot reach'. The ad that asks if you have a problem and proposes its product as the solution is one of many variations on the 'before and after' story.

Ads can tell their stories with humour, as in the Guinness ads; with drama, such as those for cars, which commonly emphasize their speed; and with emotion, like the nostalgic return to the pastoral countryside in the Hovis bread television commercials and the family in the sentimental Oxo ads.

Every story has a cast of characters. Obviously, for the most part ads offer ideal characters, beautiful people we would most like to be. There are exceptions, such as charity posters, which use images of starving people to touch our consciences and arouse us to send money, rather than to spend it. But even here, the images are chosen to fulfil a purpose, one that we recognize and know how to respond to. Charity posters, like any other form of advertising, use character types.

Famous people can be used to offer testimonials, to vouch for the quality of the product they are advertising. Their fame enables us to know at a glance the type of person they are and thereby helps to place the product for us. Eleanor Roosevelt, wife of the American President, testified for Good Luck margarine in the 1950s in much the same way as Roger Daltrey of The Who rock band testifies today for the American Express credit card. When a dispute between advertisers and the actor's union in Britain threatened television advertising in the early 1980s, some products featured testimonials from their own manu-facturers. This somewhat bizarre occurrence caught on and today the representatives from Braun shavers and OTV Video, among others, have become familiar faces.

Ads tell stories; one photograph and two lines of dialogue prompt us to fill out a story of whirlwind romance in this ad for diamonds.

"But where's your old sports car?" I asked.

"I've just put it on your finger," he laughed.

This ring, from Mappin and Webb, is set with the finest quality oval diamond of 1.23 carats, with tapered baguettes, totalling 0.70 of a carat.

The quality and value of all diamonds are judged by the 4Cs (cut, colour, clarity and carat weight) but fine diamonds like these have a special fire and brilliance.

For further information on choosing diamonds and the work of other leading diamond designers, just write to Mappin and Webb, Dept. 4a, 106 Regent Street, London W1R 6JH.

A diamond is forever

Celebrity Jerry Hall is seen to offer both a testimonial and an ideal of female glamour and beauty for a hair-care product.

33

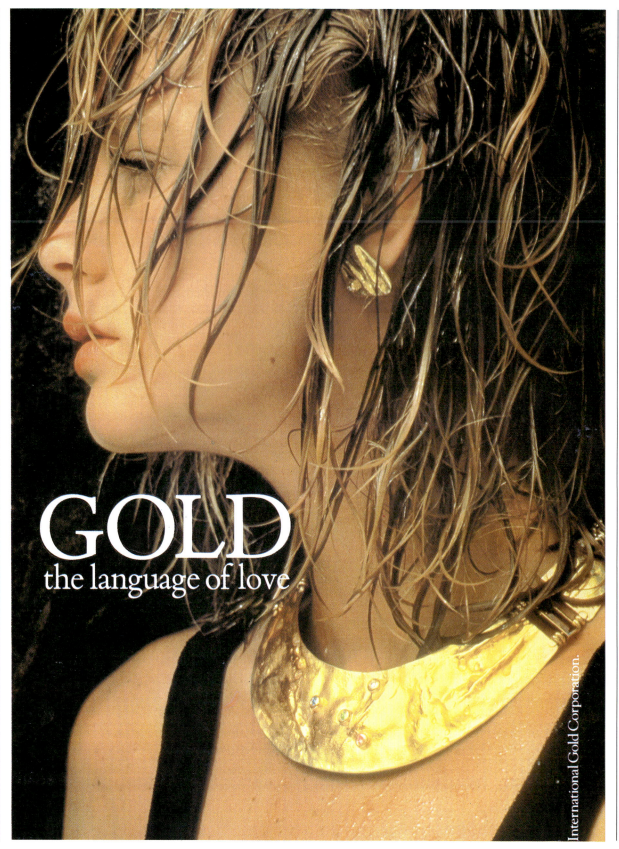

GOLD
the language of love

Most ads do not rely on famous people to sell products. Instead they use models, hired by advertising agencies to pose for photographs or act in commercials. These models fall into common types.

There are more female than male types. This should not be surprising since women are overwhelmingly the major market for advertisers. More men may control spending than women as more men are in paid (and often better paid) employment than women. But it seems that it is women who initiate spending and who actually spend much more than men. In addition, ads featuring products for women rarely feature men, whereas ads featuring products for men commonly have women in them. This tells us much about the value advertising, like society in general, places on stereotyped images of women.

There are basically two female stereotypes in advertising; the domestic type and the beauty. Images of mothers and wives sell domestic products from butter to washing machines. Images of beauty sell cosmetics and clothing. The two types rarely combine. The beauty is highly glamorized, sensuously dressed and posed to emphasize the contours of her body. Her face will most often be turned towards us, her eyes looking provocatively at us, or sometimes turned a little away with a look of intense pleasure. Ads intended for male markets commonly offer the full face of the woman, whereas female markets will usually see the profile. One reason for this is what the type is being used to suggest. She seems inviting, provocative or alluring to the male viewer, and suggests satisfaction or success in a male conquest for the female viewer. In other

Left *We are invited to find pleasure in looking — for men, in looking at, and for women, in looking like — the alluring profile of the model whose body advertises gold.*

The type of beautiful woman differs according to whether the product is mainly for men or women. The glamorous women in this ad engage the eye of the targeted reader directly.

words, men are invited to think that this woman is aroused by them as others will be when he buys the product she is advertising. Women, however, are invited to imagine that this woman is what they will be like if they buy the product she is advertising.

The use of female sexuality in advertisements is often carried out very subtly. It appears in a kind of code. Although advertisers and consumers alike know that sexual desire is a strong selling point in these ads, neither openly acknowledges it. Everyone 'gets' the point though no one makes it.

The domestic type of woman commonly

The domestic female type in an implied story about a caring mother preparing to send her son off to school, in this ad for a breakfast cereal.

shown in ads may look homely and attractive, but is rarely shown as sexually provocative. The emphasis is upon her efficiency and reliability, whether wiping tears from the eyes of a child or attacking the stains on a husband's shirt. More often than the beauty, the domestic type appears as a character in a story, acting out a drama. Rarely does she appear simply to be looked at; What she is doing is far more important.

Other female types appear much less frequently though they do exist — especially for specific female markets. Tomboys and comic characters advertise products for young women. Career women appear in up-market women's magazines and in some business journals. When types like this appear in other ads, they are more commonly used as figures of fun, usually aimed at male consumers, to suggest what women should not be. For every type, therefore, we can talk about dominant images, those that occur most frequently, and subordinate images, those that appear more rarely but that widen the range of images.

Classifying people into types is common in advertising, whether they are women or men, young or old, rich or poor, white or black. But different types appear in the same ads for different markets. The Marlboro cowboy is always white in the USA, Britain and Australia. But in African countries, he is always black. Common washing powders advertised with white models on television are advertised by black models in newspapers for black people.

The gender types — the macho male or the domestic woman — remain the same but the racial types change, according to their markets.

Of all the social types in advertising, images of women and black people have proved the most contentious; women by the limited range of images available, black people by their absence. But as the above examples demonstrate, the discussion of dominant images holds good only for certain countries and for certain markets.

In the countries of Islam, for instance, it is illegal to use photographs of women. Only line drawings are acceptable in a culture that frowns upon female sexual display. In the continental countries of Europe, however, female nudity — though not male — is common in advertising. In Britain and the USA it is not.

As well as the domestic and the glamorous stereotypes of women, advertisers sometimes use the tomboy image in an attempt to appeal to the teenage market. These advertisements are usually aimed at young women.

Above *Racial types in advertising reflect the majority racial group in any market: whites in predominantly white markets but black in black markets.*

Right *In this Japanese diamond ad there is little suggestion of a romantic liaison which contrasts with the British ad on page 32.*

National and cultural differences mean that advertising campaigns change in certain essential details as they travel across the world and into different markets. The campaign for Impulse body perfume, for instance, featured a man moved to shower flowers upon a woman wearing this perfume. In France, the woman was naked on a beach; in Britain a romantic liaison was promised; in Japan the meeting was respectable and restrained; in the Arab countries no variation was acceptable and the campaign was dropped.

What is considered acceptable advertising changes around the world. Different groups of people may even disagree with what agencies governing the regulation of advertising have themselves found acceptable. What are these regulations and who has control over them?

優美は、
あなたの上に輝く。

きょうのあなたは、ひときわまばゆい。
ひときわ私を魅きつける。
カラット・ダイヤモンド。ただひとりのために、
この世に生まれたひとつぶ。
1カラット以上の輝き、澄みきった美しさこそ
あなたにふさわしい。その光には
真に素晴らしい女性をつくる、不思議な力がある。
カラット・ダイヤモンド。

Carat Diamond
カラット・ダイヤモンド、選ばれたひとつぶ。

4C 4つのCがダイヤモンドの品質基準。
ダイヤモンドは永遠の輝き De Beers

写真の商品は1.688ct/0.75ctです。商品に関するお問い合わせは、大阪・うめだ阪急百貨店8階宝飾品サロン（E4-10係）〒530大阪市北区角田町8-7 TEL.06(361)1381〈木曜定休〉

6 Controlling advertising

Every country in the world has regulations governing advertising. There are regulations controlling how much advertising we can see and where it can be seen. Every city has by-laws prohibiting the hanging of signs and billboards where they would be out of keeping with the environment. Even advertisers recognize that too many ads cluttering up one space is counter-productive for them. Rules also govern the proportion of ads to copy in newspapers as well as the amount and timing of ads on television. Finally, there are regulations designed to ensure that claims made in ads can be justified and that the interests of consumers are protected. It is this question of 'consumer interests' that begs many more questions and which has proved most controversial.

In China and the USSR, the government controls advertising through agencies set up by the state and accountable to it. In most other countries, these agencies are more independent of government control. In Britain, two agencies publish rules for all advertisers. The first looks after the broadcast media of television and radio; it is called the Independent Broadcasting Authority (IBA). The second controls non-broadcast media, such as the press and the cinema; it is called the British Code of Advertising Practice (BCAP).

BCAP advises advertisers on their ads and campaigns, checking about 26 million display ads for posters and publications each year. Separate committees deal with new advertising for cigarettes and tobacco, slimming products and hair treatments, for example. The Code is a 72-page document which says that all ads should:
— be legal, decent, honest and truthful
— follow business principles of fair competition
— be responsible to consumers and society.
Complaints on any of these counts are dealt

Below *Who permits these billboards to be erected on this Botswana street? Who controls what can be said on the posters? Every country has organizations responsible for these matters.*

Right *The Advertising Standards Authority is the organization in Britain that receives complaints about advertising and adjudicates on them on behalf of the public.*

If an advertisement is wrong, we're here to put it right.

The Advertising Standards Authority. ✔

ASA Ltd., Brook House, Torrington Place, London WC1E 7HN.

with by the Advertising Standards Authority (ASA). It regularly publishes details of complaints received and the results of its investigations. Advertisers who refuse to amend or withdraw ads that have broken with the Code can be barred from advertising in any medium.

The IBA oversees a Broadcasting Act of 1981 which affects advertising on independent television and local radio. The Act requires the IBA to:

—exclude from broadcasting any ad which is likely to mislead
—draw up and review the Code of Advertising Standards and Practice
—ensure that advertisers comply with the Code.

Over 12,000 commercials are checked each year to judge if the claims they make are true, if they offend good taste or decency or if they may be offensive to the public.

These agencies, commonly called 'watchdogs', have their counterparts in other countries. In the USA, for instance, the National Advertising Review Board is the equivalent of BCAP. The National Association of Broadcasters is similar to the IBA and the Federal Trade Commission prosecutes for deception in the same way as the ASA.

As well as making rules that apply to all advertising, these regulating authorities have special rules that apply to ads for children. No ad must be harmful or make potentially dangerous suggestions. For the most part, everyone would agree that any ad suggesting

Steve Bell's Guardian *strip cartoon satirizes Coca Cola's TV ad in which a large theatre is filled with international youth singing in harmony.*

the sort of behaviour that puts the life or health of adults or children at risk — such as jumping from a great height or putting a plastic bag over your head — should not be allowed. But beyond such clear-cut examples lies confusion and argument.

Should films or television programmes for children be allowed, for instance, if they are connected to the sale of related goods? The film *Star Wars* was massively popular and made worldwide rentals of over $400 million in 1984. Other films in the series made nearly twice that amount. But these figures are as nothing to the profits made from merchandizing the Star Wars characters and machines as toys. Today, many films, pop records, television programmes and fashions are connected in ways that sell each other as well as other goods in one grand design.

Television cartoon series featuring characters sold as soft toys are now regularly offered at no cost to the television channels. Each time they are screened they act as hidden advertising for goods sold in the shops. Popular cartoon series like *My Little Pony, Care Bears* and *Thundercats* fall into this category.

So far, advertising authorities have turned a blind eye to this kind of hidden advertising. But this has not stopped some parents' groups and moralist lobbies from claiming such forms of advertising to be harmful to the interests of the consumer. Clearly, what can be argued as harmful and against a consumer's interests is open to debate.

Similarly, many women object to the narrow, stereotyped images of themselves used in ads, which they find offensive; they, too, have a notion of 'harm', and feel that their interests as

Star Wars' *villain Darth Vader, like other characters in the film, was used to advertise a vast range of children's toys.*

women consumers are not being met.

The problem for the regulating authorities is that there are competing claims to consumer's interests which rely on conflicting definitions. If you have a complaint about the accuracy of an ad, it is likely to be dealt with sympathetically. Likewise, if your complaint concerns offences against taste and decency, you will certainly be heard. But for more sophisticated objections from minority social groups, there is much less likelihood of satisfaction.

There are, therefore, competing claims by different groups of consumers. But there is also a degree of self-interest in the groups who regulate advertising, since they are so closely related to the industry itself. Although these authorities staff their panels with many experts, few who are independent of the advertising industry are represented; in the end they are accountable only to themselves.

Groups who have complained to an advertising authority about images of themselves which they have found offensive get very angry when their complaint is refused. Sometimes they feel that the only action left to

An information poster from a campaign objecting to sexist advertising that uses women's bodies to sell unrelated products, especially to men.

them in such circumstances is to deface posters with graffiti. This is a criminal offence, however, and people have been arrested for it. Some people have become so incensed by advertising that they have organized their own campaigns to stop the offending ads, often with success.

The rules that govern the regulation of advertising have changed over time, just as advertising itself has changed. They will doubtless change in the future, too, in accordance with pressure from increasing numbers of people: today's minority campaign could become tomorrow's regulations.

Until very recently companies that manufactured contraceptives were forbidden to advertise. Now public anxiety over the terrible deaths caused by the AIDS virus have changed all that — at least advertising for condoms is now common.

"I EXPECT TO GET THROUGH 50 GROSS IN THE NEXT FEW MONTHS."

Glossary

Account A person or company paying for the services of an advertising agency; a client.

Advertorial News 'stories' paid for by advertisers.

Artwork The design or the visual element of an ad.

Audience People grouped together to watch a performance; used here to describe how people use advertising for purposes other than as consumers.

Body The written text or copy of an ad.

Brand image An idea advertisers seek to associate with a brand.

Brand name The name of a product, eg Oxo, Yorkie.

Campaign An organized package of ads produced by an agency for an advertiser; a plan of action by any group.

Character types Familiar social types in advertising illustrations and elsewhere; eg women as mothers.

Classified Small ads in newspapers.

Commercial A television advertisement.

Competitor A company advertising a product similar to another but under another brand name.

Copy The written text of an ad, also termed the body.

Consumer A person who buys or is intended to buy a product advertised.

Consumer interests A contentious term describing what a group, lobby or advertising regulating agency assert as their interests as consumers.

Creative director Senior worker in an advertising agency responsible for managing a campaign for a client.

Display ad A printed ad separated from articles usually by being boxed in.

Dominant images Types that appear most commonly in ads and elsewhere.

Graphics Visual designs incorporating lettering, tables, bar charts, etc.

Headline The largest lines of type in an ad, usually an eye-catching slogan.

Hoarding A large structure for siting poster ads on roadsides and city streets; in the USA usually called a billboard.

Jingle A few lines of song or a tune identifying an ad.

Lobby A group of people who gather together to put pressure on an organization that has power to make changes.

Market A social group targeted as consumers for a product by advertisers.

Market research The collection of information about actual or potential markets acquired by interviews, tests, questionnaires, etc.

Posting Putting posters on hoardings or other advertising sites.

Product identification An idea advertisers want consumers to identify with a product.

Product positioning The indication in the brand image of the intended market for a product.

Profit The sum of money left over from the selling price of a product after its production cost has been deducted.

Rates Charges made by the media for space and time in newspapers, or on television.

Slogan The main lines of copy selling a product.

Space Space in a publication bought for advertising.

Sponsorship Companies who sponsor a television programme or other event by paying for or towards the costs of it.

Testimonials Advertising that features a famous person who vouches for the product.

Target audience The group of consumers aimed at by an advertising campaign.

Typeface/typography The style of lettering used in advertising design.

Unequal relationship A relationship in which one person or group has more power to act than another.

Voice-over The commentary of an unseen speaker in a commercial.

Booklist

Advertising Association *Finding out . . . About Advertising* An introductory booklet sympathetic to the advertising industry and containing colourful examples of campaigns.

BFI Education *Selling Pictures* (British Film Institute, 1983) This teaching pack contains a student booklet called *The Companies You Keep* which provides an excellent analysis of advertising among its many other resources.

Gillian Dyer *Advertising as Communication* (Methuen, 1982) A good critical book for sixth form and older students.

Erving Goffman *Gender Advertisements* (Macmillan, 1979) A well illustrated analysis of body positions in ads and what they mean.

Sally Henderson and Robert Landau *Billboard Art* (Angus & Robertson, 1981) A well illustrated history of American billboard posters.

Kathy Myers *Understains* (Comedia, 1986) A critical account of the main arguments concerning advertising.

David Ogilvy *Ogilvy on Advertising* (Pan, 1983) An illustrated guide to the industry by one of the USA's leading advertisers.

Jill Posener *Spray it Loud* (Routledge & Kegan Paul, 1982) An amusing collection of photographs of graffiti.

Scottish Film Council *Baxters* (1985) A simulation of how a campaign is organized. It includes visual material and a video tape.

Valerie Thom *Advertising* (Edward Arnold, 1980) A simple and critical beginners guide.

E. S. Turner *The Shocking History of Advertising* (Penguin, 1952) A slightly dated but very thorough history which, although written for adults, has a very readable style.

Further Information

For posters, leaflets and information about the advertising industry, write to the following:

Advertising Association
Abford House
15 Wilton Road
London SW1V 1NJ

The Cinema Advertising Association
127 Wardour Street
London W1V 4AD

To complain about an ad, write to:

Advertising Standards Authority
Brook House
2-16 Torrington Place
London WC1E 7HN

Independent Broadcasting Authority
70 Brompton Road
London SW3 1EY

To obtain the classroom materials mentioned in the booklist:

British Film Institute
81 Dean Street
London W1V 6AA

The Scottish Film Council
Dowanhill
74 Victoria Crescent Road
Glasgow G12 9JN

Index

Picture acknowledgements

The author and publishers would like to thank the following for allowing their illustrations to be reproduced in this book: the Advertising Standards Authority 41; Aquarius Picture Library 43 (top); Steve Bell 42; DDB Needham (Bryant & May) 27; DMB&B (Maxwell House) 19; Diamond Information Centre 33, 39; Esso 22, 23 (both); Mary Evans Picture Library 10, 11; Format Photographers 8; GLC 43 (bottom); Greenpeace 17; the Hutchison Library 18, 38, 40; McCann Erickson (Nescafé) 20, (L'Oreal) 33, 35; National Film Archive 15; Peter Newark's Western Americana 9; Christine Osborne 26; Rex Features 7; Still Price Court Twivy D'Souza (Mates) 44; J. Walter Thompson (Benetton) 21, 37, (Andrex) 30; Topham 6; Malcolm S. Walker 4, 24 (both); Woolworths PLC 25 (both); ZEFA 5, 16. All other pictures supplied by the Wayland Picture Library.